A Journey *into the* Mind *of a* POET

— TEARLE MONETTE —

NEWMAN SPRINGS PUBLISHING
320 Broad Street
Red Bank, NJ 07701

First originally published by Newman Springs Publishing 2024

ISBN 979-8-89308-678-2 (Paperback)
ISBN 979-8-89308-679-9 (Digital)

Printed in the United States of America

To Thelma

BEAUTIFUL

It's not easy to write a poem for someone as beautiful as you are. Maybe it's your smile that could bring sunshine to every dark cloud that's embedded inside a man's soul, purifying his body with true love. Or maybe it's your voice, so sweet and powerful, yet so caring, with a touch of your demands molding you both inside and out. It forms that beauty from within. So keep your head up. Sometimes the rain can weather the storm; in the eye of it all is where you don't belong. Just by the way you walk, the motion of your body pours out positivity and confidence in your soul. Is that's why they say your beauty shows when you glow? The outer you is not a reflection of your inner being. The skin we see is just an image, an accent of your beauty. I guess it was easy after all to write a poem for someone as beautiful as you are.

I'VE MADE HER VOICE SING

Part 1

We're both in this bed; no one's talking because of the argument we just had (a relationship love song). It puts a wedge between our bodies, making us feel so far away. I'm tossing, she's turning, we both can't get any sleep. Our bodies feel cold with these unwanted feelings. I don't like this feeling. Our souls need that physical touch. So I took away the pillow that was a border between us and gently got on top of her, with my warm and soft hands rubbing her inner thighs. That's when she opened her legs and then her eyes. They connected to mine with a tender kiss that reminded us of our very first time. Our heartbeats start racing. With my slow thrusts, her motion sinks me deeper into her love potion, and we both can't control this passion. That's something we can't escape from. Just when we thought we were pushing away the fire which brought forth the desire, I've made her voice sing.

YOU NEED ME

I can't hide the way I feel inside; your eyes and mine pretending to be shy. I've made my move so I was first to try. You put up a front by keeping real deep feelings inside. By trying not to be weak, or is it fear? I know your last relationship put you in a standstill. So is that the reason why you try to hide because you were bound by fear? That battle you're fighting seems to be strong, but I am here with you; you're not alone. I've put aside my pride so I can share your cries. Putting you first became my sacrifice. My love is unmatched with these good intentions, so you can let go of past pain and start to remember our future dreams instead of your own acceptance of misery based on your own disbeliefs. Betting on things that you can't see got you blinded to the truth that you need me.

BELIEVE

My mind gets to wondering if I am doing the right things because I never took the time to sort out my pain and the pain that was given to me. It intertwines with one another like a ball of yarn; I really don't know which one is pulling the strings. To truly be free and to find peace in our insanity, it takes a strong person to admit their wrongs and to rebuild themselves from the ground up. Also because of this, life gets confusing sometimes, this unbalanced scale of time making us fear the unknown, so it stops the blessing inside. We're blinded from the path that was certain, so focused on the comfort in the pain that was chosen, despite all the warning signs. The red light was bright enough to penetrate our thoughts, so the process is blocked. It's time to heal and lean on your own faith by understanding that I am not my mistakes. Let go and try to conceive that it's all in God's plan; we just got to believe.

SPENDING MY TIME

You came into my life when I was rich in spirit. See, I've moved forward and left my demons. I had to spend some of my time to get into this position and didn't want to waste any more. Now I've got you, and all you're doing is spending it with all these lies after lies, subtracting my time. I can't focus on mine. You're holding me down; this weight is too heavy for my shoulders. It wasn't there before because you've been selfish, lightening your load just to control my time. You've got me paying for something I didn't do; you brought it with you. Your problems are consuming my hours, turning into minutes into seconds, spending my time. You've got me giving up my lifeline for depression.

FEAR THE FEEL

You're not for real. Too many games because you'd rather fear the feel. I've pumped up your life—what a hard price—because I didn't know better. I helped pull you out of that fire. Now it's slowly burning me. Your mind is gone; it seems that you don't care. All you know is pain, and you're taking me there. I've peeled away your lies, uncovered the truth inside. Your fear planted a seed that grew a vine covering your heart so you can't feel mine. This is your protector; you've been hurt too many times. The very thought of you letting it go will make you vulnerable toward something you can't come back from, so you're rationing out your affection to keep your emotions safe. See, I know you now. You're holding on to fear; your cries don't share the same tears as mine. I just don't know why you won't change this feel. I've wasted all these years because you'd rather fear the feel.

SACRIFICE

You came to me when I was at my best; you were down and out, so you became my test. I'm up in the air, flying so high, looked down and saw your broken wings, so I decided to break mine. Now I am on land. The air is heavy down here, and it's heavy on the heart. It's weighing me down; now my feet are touching the ground that you embark on, causing me to realize that I can't go back where I came from. I'm stuck with you, and as long as you make room for me, I will make room for you. Your loneliness has me confined. So no matter how hard it gets, our trials and tribulations are a test just to see how strong our love can get. I've let go of my own selfish reasons. Focus on your soul because it needs some healing. You've become my soulmate, and I can't leave you. So when time is not on our side, just don't leave me behind, because now I'm crawling so you can walk. This is my sacrifice.

MY DAYS ARE NIGHTS,
MY NIGHTS ARE DAYS

My days are nights; my nights are days. Nothing seems to be the same. Separated from my thoughts and pride, splitting my soul so I can enjoy the sinful spoils of life, but what about the light? Just a flash, a flicker in your eyes, seems so small to you because you don't care. I guess it's my emotions taking you for a ride there. My days, I can't sleep; my nights, I'm awake. Frontward walking, at least that's what I think because I keep going back to where time relapses, where wet cement sinks—a dream or is it reality? I'm not sure, caught up with the notice of not knowing if I'm coming or going, being confused from it all. The purpose of remembering is to remind ourselves where we came from. Trying to forget and to move on got us struggling between right and wrong, slipping this mind into a black hole of the abyss, lost in a wandering mind so it won't escape. My days are nights, and my nights are days. Nothing to me seems real or feels the same.

WHAT A LONELY
PLACE TO BE

I've made you alone in this place because I feel alone. This is not the love I wanted, so I don't see where I belong. Blocking your feelings just to tell you mine, now I'm battling you just to show you who really hurts the most inside, not knowing that you might be the one for me. I've treated you badly with no remorse, apologizing quickly, but this man is moving quickly, dodging your love spears because someone else has a target on my feelings. Took my smile and threw away my tears. I am so sorry for inviting fear, but my love belongs to someone else here. Yet you keep coming around, showing me love felt deeply. Don't get me wrong; I won't change a thing about you. Your caring is unmatched; any man would want you. But this is what you need to feel from me instead of me giving you a blank invitation to love. What a lonely place to be.

I'VE LOST MY WAY

What happened to me? I've lost my way, walking, looking like someone's behind me. Taking baby steps so I can hear someone creeping, I'm spellbound, controlled by different feelings. I can't shake this. The lights are on, but darkness surrounds me. It got me second-guessing how strong my demons are because they've got me on the ropes, and I am looking skinny. Yeah, malnutrition because I'm not eating; pain and depression are in my life—that's what feeds me. What happened to me? I've lost my way. Where do I go from here without a clue? Plus, some of the stuff I can't remember. It went in one ear and out the other. Now my mind is stuck in a protection stage, making it harder for me to formulate a plan. So I look to the sky with my piercing eyes, penetrating the clouds of heaven, trying to get God's attention because my angels are not helping. I guess it's my fault because I've stopped listening. I've lost my way.

ONE'S SOUL

The spaces between our minds are either trapped or erased through time, which makes us so scared to go forward because we can't see the invisible lines. It's what we can't see that makes one's reality turn the pages of our own disbelief. We're all on borrowed time, so my soul can't shed its own skin, so it's sharing mine. What our bodies want and what we can't see is our souls wanting to lean on faith; we just aren't listening. We're like slaves; our minds can't break it. We imprison our souls so they won't escape from the pain that we cause, too busy consuming the bittersweet of reality to even give it a thought. Our minds battle the spoils of war, which creates a rift between our bodies and souls. Or is it much safer to bottle it all in than to release the pain that's poisoning within one's soul?

MYSELF

I've seen myself within myself, knowing that I need to change. I've put myself inside a box, locked up so that I can hide the pain. It's a shame we turn our backs to the needy just to endure and feed those blinded by greed, so that we can get lost and lose ourselves in their own misery. Because of that, I'm running, not looking back. My clock just keeps on ticking. You hurt me; I hurt myself, and I'm the only one who's grieving. That makes me pull to the left because I don't know what's right. What a battle I must conquer. It has gotten me too scared to open up—too many keyholes, don't know which one I can unlock and set myself free. Maybe if I take my time, I can find the right one instead of being stuck. Got me trapped with these chains that bound me. I'm myself; I love myself—that's what I keep saying to myself because self can't change self alone without myself holding on to help carry this load.

STEPS

I am hearing footsteps behind me, getting closer. I started to walk faster, but they're keeping up with my motion. Every turn that I make, the footsteps keep up the pace. So focused on those steps, I am forgetting how to step. My calculated mind is frozen in time, in a state of shock, wondering who's stepping behind me in the dark. Maybe it's my past trying to catch up with me—the troubles of a child or a misunderstood teen, both of which I left behind to fulfill this dream. You know, leaving that half of myself so my life can be easy. It didn't do anything but keep them closer to me. No wonder I don't feel whole; I left behind a piece of me. It made it seem that I was scared—the fragile part of me I didn't want to share—because I thought that no one would care to listen to a grown man's pain. That's what left my steps unbalanced because of the shame.

FORGIVENESS

It's a lot that we keep inside, figuring that we might be weak if we relieve it. The strength is the fire; I guess we find pleasure in the darkest hours, believing anything that comes with a desire. But it's our pleasure that gives us our pressure points; we need to relieve them. Let's start by painting a picture of the ones who gave us misery, so we can remember and move on to a fresh paint of memories by filtering out unwelcome feelings and leaving the wanted feelings, putting ourselves in a stronger position to fight unnecessary vengeance so we can accept and let in forgiveness.

CRAZY

Never gave myself happiness; giving it to you has controlled these thoughts like raindrops falling on a one-sided road (crazy). Tugging at the fabric of desire, looking but not seeing that this love has expired. I still want you though (crazy). Being the best man became too perfect for someone who just wants no energy. It's weakened a man like me to the point that I don't care what you do to me (crazy). I want to leave you, but you've got too much invested in me. See, this man's pride puts reality to the side; now we're both playing silly games (crazy). This has to be one of the strangest things—forcing you into a love that you weren't ready for had you creating a strong hate toward me. But I'd rather live in your wants than have you leave me because maybe one day you will learn to love me. That is crazy.

THIS SHADOW OF LIGHT

This shadow of light peeping through my cracked window, I'm hearing a voice saying, "No more." Laying here with my eyes cracked open, seeing a glimpse of light and a person, she's hitting me with volts. It's keeping my body from closing. There's not much for me to do but wait to see who will win. Finding myself losing and catching my wind. Lord, this hurts; I can't take it anymore. I am hearing a voice in my ear telling me to come back, stay strong. I am trying to respond, but I keep slipping further away and am confused as to why I can't feel my feet. I'm falling into a deep sleep. No sound I am hearing, without pain, in this I found peace. A woman says, "We're losing him," and hits me with more volts. It feels like lightning bolts. I'm fading quickly; this is my last hope. I've fought longer than expected. All I can see is a shadow of light peeping through my cracked window. I'm hearing a woman's voice saying, "No more."

HAS COME TO PASS

I don't understand why things had to come to pass. It has changed the fabric of my life because now it's all rearranged. It has taken my young age to understand my gray days just to see all the mistakes I've made. I am paying a price, but it was the remembering of good that was putting up a fight that saved my life. It's a struggle for me because of the hurt from the pain planted and is controlling my forgetful thinking. There are a lot of things I wish not to forget, but this disease is causing my brain to slip. I don't know who's coming to see me; their faces and names are someone else's history, leaving me wondering how this can be. They look at me like my memories are drifting like a lost boat in the middle of the ocean, and it's coinciding with my empty thoughts. My mind is like puzzle pieces that are scattered in the dark. My mind—I am losing it fast; everything that I've remembered has come to pass.

THE DAY I'LL STOP GIVING

The day I'll stop giving will be the day I'll stop breathing. You hurt me; I'll still give. It makes me feel unimportant, and I'll still give. I am small in your eyes, and I still gave you everything. See, you don't see my love; I want you to feel it. It hurts me so bad that I can't stop giving. Why can't you feel me? I won't stop giving. I'll stop breathing first because it just feels right to show you I'm for real here. But you're still talking at me instead of talking to me; I'll still give. Straight disrespect me in front of my family and friends; I'll still give. See, I'm blinded by the little things you do for me. It's not a lot when you've never had much, and you're using it to your advantage. A fool, I fell in love but am confused as to why you're laughing. The day I'll stop giving will be the day I'll stop...

ADDICTION

I didn't know how weak I'd become because if I knew how weak then maybe I wouldn't have inhaled ill thoughts through me. It's dangerous, so I put poison in me just to ease the pain. Now I am using it to get through the day. These seasons have paused. Where did I go? I've lied to myself; I'm not in control. But the very thought of losing it won't let me go through life without it. Because if I don't get it, I'll fall back into an infant stage of thinking—my cries of wants for the need until I get it by any means necessary. Stealing 'cause it's necessary. I am bonded by the temporary feeling it's giving me, my only friend understanding me emotionally. Controlled like a puppet, this drug is the string that guides me to a sunken place, trapped in my own body. What have I just created? I've become my worst enemy. The darkness overcomes my light, which brought forth a demon. I've tried to fight it by trying to hide it, but I'll be so sick without it. This is why I move around and keep my distance. So let me introduce you to my addiction.

SON FROM A MOTHER'S TEARS

I know I wasn't the best son that I could have been. I am sorry. Never listened to your problems. Forgive me. I thought I had all the answers, trying to solve it, so stupid of me to leave you out and not tell you my feelings. So when things started to fall apart, I blamed you just to tell you that I'm doing too much to figure it out, trying to have you consume the guilt of evil. My fault. Because I was too scared to face my own demons. Giving it all to you seemed so simple, not realizing the hurt of guilt my indulgence endured you by changing the fabric that was woven between son and mother. That's what hurts the most because it's not fair to have you standing there thinking you didn't do your best, so my sins became your test. In the thick of it all, thank you, Mom, for being real. When things were foggy, through your eyes it was made clearer. That's why I can float here and deal with my fears because I am her son from a mother's tears.

THE DARKEST SIDE OF ME

I can remember those days when I lived carefree and free, never heard nor felt this thing we call grieving. Maybe I was simple-minded, blinded by those simple times when hate wasn't forced to destroy a man's soul, only to turn around and curse the very things that he spoils. From a man who didn't understand the true meaning of love until the shame came in, and I couldn't cry because my pain turned into anger from losing two children. I never knew that things could get even worse until I couldn't see any more smiles coming from my baby sister. I am trying not to lose it, but it's hard for me to pay attention. I've lost my auntie and my son's grandmother in the same sentence. I know they're up in heaven; peace and love are surrounding them. Even though my heart is pure, it's the pain that endures. Is this my defense to protect what's left of my innocence? Because I'm starting to pull more to the darkest side, the feeling I'm receiving is not a feeling of pleasure but being numb, if that's a feeling. Is it shutting everything down that can ease me, or is it a protector that is a projection of my own creation? It seems to me that the darkest side of me came to bring peace, but people might say it's my enemy.

ENEMY

I've always fought for others, but never fought for myself; it left an empty place where my heart rests. Always putting myself last regardless of the stress. Saying I'll be okay left me borderline crazy. Don't know who I'm looking at when I'm in the mirror, a reflection of presumably someone else's doing, has gotten me not recognizing my facial features. Now I am in a rage, hating myself for allowing me to be controlled this way. I've shown love even on those rainy days, but under my umbrella, I still didn't feel safe. Don't know who's to blame; is it me or you, or is it one and the same? This very thing is destroying the innocence in me because of the shame. The lies I tell myself, using them as a crutch, are sealing my fate. All the love I've shown, was it a waste? Because it came out the other end with hate. Now that I am lost, will someone save me from me? Don't like what I'm seeing. I've become my worst enemy.

BLIND MEN CRIES

You've got me feeling that uncertain feel; I can't see your facial expression because you stay on one look like a statue with no emotion, rubbing my eyes so I can stay focused. It just doesn't work, too blurry for my vision because I can't read you clearly. You want me, then you don't. Your lies became the trust which has me low to myself, so I can't see, not paying attention to the signs, the blurred lines that they speak. Trying to look through you is like a dirty glass. What's inside is a mystery; got me questioning what I am missing. Someone else has your full attention, the singing and the happiness that you process, the silence of guilt is what I get. I have to sit down now because I am starting to feel weak; your cupid shot poison arrows through me, that's what blinded me. It hurts because I can't look at you the same with tears falling from my eyes; this is a blind man's cry.

INTO THE MOUTH
OF MADNESS

Just can't talk to you like I care; I'd rather yell at you because you don't care, curse you out, call you every name but good, grabbing you, shaking you until you understand what I'm doing. Words can hurt, and I'm giving it to you. Feeding you with guilt until your belly gets full. You want me to see you, but I'm looking straight through you. I'm not in the mood to be juggling with my inner self because it wants me to defuse. So I just won't feel you, and see right past you, stomping your feet, yelling out loud, saying it's my fault for being a clown, hitting the wall with my fists, putting the blame where it fits. I guess we both blame each other; this relationship can't be fixed. You scream, I scream, you yell, I yell, you don't care while biting your bottom lip. Welcome into the mouth of madness.

THE ROAD WE MUST TRAVEL TO (REDEMPTION)

I told myself today is the day that I will move forward. Being so stuck in the past has gotten me out of sync. Everybody moved on and left me in a hurry, and they left me with my own problems on my shoulders. A changed man I thought I'd never be, so much wrong I've done turned me into my worst enemy. Now I'm standing here on this road, and I'm cold, blowing hot air onto my hands just to keep warm. This road is hard to travel alone, too many bad memories of things I've done. I have to rewrite my wrongs. That was caused by people who have done me wrong, walking backward just to faint, waking up as a blind man who's walking forward toward faith. So this is how it feels to overthink, cramming so many thoughts in my mind that my legs can't even motivate. To travel this way takes believing in yourself. The road seems far, but we will get there like a turtle that believes it can win a race. Don't look back, even if it's tempting, because this road I'm on is traveling to redemption.

A JOURNEY INSIDE THE MIND OF A POET

She was so BEAUTIFUL, so I MADE HER VOICE SING, looked into her eyes, and said YOU NEED ME. JUST BELIEVE me, I'm SPENDING MY TIME, but you'd rather FEAR THE FEEL, so I SACRIFICE, and MY DAYS ARE NIGHTS now. WHAT A LONELY PLACE TO BE. I have been hurt so much that I'VE LOST MY WAY. Loving ONE'S SOUL had me taking STEPS toward FORGIVENESS. Is it CRAZY looking at this SHADOW OF LIGHT peeping through my cracked window? Or has it COME TO PASS because THE DAY I'LL STOP GIVING will be my first ADDICTION? I'm a SON OF MY MOTHER'S TEARS, so that makes me lean on THE DARKEST SIDE OF ME because MY ENEMY blinded this MAN'S CRIES. INTO THE MOUTH OF MADNESS, on my knees, screaming out real loud, "What's left for me!?" I guess it's THE ROAD WE ALL MUST TRAVEL TO REDEMPTION. This was a journey inside the mind of a poet.

ABOUT THE AUTHOR

He lived a silent and shy life for half of his life and didn't know how to express the things he was seeing and feeling, so he kept it bottled up inside. Until now, he has found a voice.